A 40-DAY JOURNAL OF
RADIANT REVELATIONS

RANDI MEACHAM

Dedication

I dedicate this book to my beautiful brown granddaughters in all of their glorious shades of splendor. Stand tall Harmony, Brandi, and Italy. Your beauty is unmatched! Stay true, my princesses, your very existence is truth! I dedicate this book to my sons, my kings, Brandon, Jalen, and Shawn and to my one and only grandson, Eric. You are the continuation of the seed. Through you our name continues, walk boldly in your calling and carry on with dignity. I dedicate this book to the love of my life, my soulmate, Elritt Meacham III. Thank you for being a man of strength and dignity and for answering the call to love me as Christ loves the set apart. Even in my brokenness, you stuck it out. Thank you, my good man! And last but certainly not least, I dedicate this book to my mother, Norma Jean. You reign forever in my heart, beautiful queen! I wear your crown with honor. I imagine you sitting at the Father's feet now, donning your glorified body, resting in your mansion... Cheering me on! "Yan, tell them that Elohim really does love them. Tell them that His love is perfect and that it casts out fear! That they REALLY are fearfully and wonderfully made and that He wants them to know it very well. Remind them that He has prepared a place for them and that it's even more glorious than they can ever imagine. Tell them that

Randi Meacham

He came that they may have life, an abundant life, not just in paradise, but on earth as well!"

I rise up and call her blessed!

My Story

The sun shined brighter on March 18, 2017. It had been fourteen days since she had transitioned to eternity. I resolved to honor her wishes: "To blow her ashes in the wind." My best friend, my mother... was now gone! Mere ashes were all that remained of her seventy years of life. Hers was a complicated life, riddled with successes and failures, highs and far too many lows. A saved soul but a soul never accepting of the freedom that salvation afforded. As a child, I often watched her intently not quite old enough to understand intellectually, what my spirit comprehended undeniably. We were bound together in more ways than one, mother and daughter biologically but sisters in spirit. There was a missing link to both of our existences. A piece of our puzzles somehow lost in the maze of a complicated life. She was always so very meticulously put together. Picture perfect on the outside but shattered on the inside, form without function! Many of her decisions were woefully reflective of her insecurities, an identity crisis always on the verge of an all-out war within. She was reared in a family of dysfunction; the mishmash of neglect and abandonment produced within her the perfect recipe for a life of reckless abandon. She was unwittingly drafted into the war of life. Bravely, she accepted the call, one enlistment after the other. She struggled, she fought and she persevered. She was a soldier at heart and it was that very heart that placed her on the battlefield in the fight for her life. It was a cold January day when she received the diagnosis of congestive heart failure. Triple bypass surgery, the cardiologist explained, was the only recourse. She tightened up her boot straps and for five long years, she fought! One thousand eight hundred and twenty five days is a long time to fight for even the most valiant warriors.

I entered the Intensive care unit, the place which had become her war room. She lay there so peacefully, helpless. I hoped, wished, and desperately prayed that she would pull through just as she had done so many times before. All the years of heartache and pain were reflective on her face. Tubes encapsulated her tiny frame, a heartbreaking reminder of a life bound by strongholds.

A ventilator breathed for this women suffocated by depression, shame, and condemnation.

An IV dripping Propofol into her veins numbed her physical pain in a way that her soul never found relief.

Rocuronium rendered her to a state of paralysis, very reminiscent of the relationships that she sought, yet never found validation in. Her oxygen levels struggled to maintain a normal rate, the numbers forever etched in my brain, 98 then 88, then 68. I'd witnessed her struggle to keep her head above water all of my life. The hustle was daunting and continuous, and sometimes victorious. I knew in that moment, I had been chosen. Full circle, I was her source of strength now, if only for a moment in time. All of the love and attention that she so desperately longed for in life, I resolved to shower upon her in the moments preceding her imminent death. I wouldn't, I couldn't leave her side. Her mother had, her father had, and all of her tumultuous relationships had. I brushed her hair, rubbed her beautifully soft skin. I felt her presence, convinced that she felt mine. I read to her, recalling in my mind the horrific stories of her childhood, suspecting that she'd never been read to before. I prayed for her, even sang her lullabies. "You are my sunshine, my only sunshine. You make me happy when skies are gray, you'll never know dear how much I love you; please don't take my sunshine away." And then a cloud appeared and with it, a hail storm of life-altering words.

"There's nothing else that we can do."

As we prepared to remove the ventilation, the nurses began to remove the IV's with hopes of her regaining consciousness. I longed for her to know that her family was by her side. I desperately wanted her to know that as she transitioned to eternity, we were there to bid her farewell. I wanted her to leave this earth knowing that she was loved, that she was appreciated, and that her life mattered. Her eyes opened. She was dazed but aware. I said, "Momma, if you understand me, squeeze my hand or blink your eyes. She struggled to squeeze my hand and then she blinked. "I love you, baby girl, and I'm here!" She blinked again with tears welling up in her eyes. "Your grandsons are here, your family is here. One by one, they acknowledged her: she blinked to acknowledge them. As the tears continued to flow, I couldn't help but believe that on her deathbed, she finally knew that she made a difference, that because she lived, we live. That our very existence was due to the fact that she struggled and fought, and through tremendous adversity, she persevered.

The nurses asked that we leave the room as they removed the ventilator. The longest three minutes of my life passed before they summoned us back into the room. She lay there, appearing so helpless, yet so strong. Struggling for air, every breath calculated. In my gut-wrenching pain, I could only think of how blessed I was to experience this moment and how I would conjure up every ounce of strength that I had in me to lovingly usher her into eternity. I placed my head upon her chest. Our eyes connected on a level so deep that it could only be described as divine. "Momma," I said, "I love you, and I am so very proud of you. I'm proud of your strength, I'm proud of your courage, I'm proud that you are my mom. It's okay, baby girl, go get your glorified body and tell Jerry that we said hello." She took three breathes and exchanged her pain for paradise. I watched in awe, as the woman who gave me life, depart from this life. She witnessed my first breath; I witnessed her last.

Forty is the number of testing. According to Scripture, the children of Israel wandered in the wilderness forty years. Elohim instructed Noah to build an ark that ultimately saved him and his family from earth's destruction by flood which lasted forty days and forty nights. The

Messiah was tempted by Satan after fasting in the wilderness for forty days.

I, too, wondered for forty years! I wondered who my father was. Why was I rejected? Who am I? I wondered until my 40th birthday. My mother sat me down and spoke the words that forever changed my life, "The man who you thought was your father, is not." For most, this revelation would have been heartbreaking, but for me, it was one of the most liberating moments of my life! I do belong! I have an identity! It all made sense! The man that I thought was my father didn't hate me. He just couldn't love me. He wasn't supposed to; I'm not his! Anger and resentment could have festered within me, anger should have been the logical response, but I was as happy for my mother as I was for myself. The yoke had been lifted. She no longer had to carry the burden of guilt and shame. I'm forever grateful for my mother's bravery. I'm certain that the secret of shame held her captive much longer than she would have wished for. She's free now, I'm free now. I pray that this 40 Day Journal of Radiant Revelations will start you on your journey towards freedom!

Day 1

Dear Soul Woman

◆

But I say, walk by the Spirit, and you will not carry out the desire of the flesh. For the flesh sets its desire against the Spirit, and the Spirit against the flesh; for these are in opposition to one another, so that you may not do the things that you please.

Galatians 5:16-17

◆

Dear Soul Women,

You're no longer in control. You're much too temperamental and cannot be trusted. Cold one day, hot the next. You're either in control or outrageously complex! You no longer have unlimited access over our emotions, you've made too many bad decisions. You will no longer deceive us into believing that our identity lies in people or possessions. The boundaries have been established. We now know that our identity lies solely in the one who laid down His life for us. Your lease is up. The Holy Spirit has taken up residence and forever dwells within us. You have been silenced. We will attentively listen to the Holy Spirit's direction. Where He leads, we will follow. We know when to speak and when to be silent. We know who to embrace and who to avoid. We will try the spirits by the Spirit, and if it's not of

Elohim, we'll conclude that it's not for us. We will discern, not compete. We will navigate through life intentionally. We will rise up, show up, and never give up! We proclaim less of us and all of Elohim!

Have a Radiant Day!

Randi Meacham

Day 2

She No Longer Lives There

◆

Therefore if anyone is in Christ, he is a
new creature; the old things passed
away; behold, new things have come.
2 Corinthians 5:17

◆

If you're looking for her, she no longer lives there! She no longer dwells in that fragile, broken space where the foundation was shaky and the walls were caving in. She moved out of that cold, dark place where the doors were locked. She escaped the prison that barred her from breaking out and others from coming in. No, she doesn't live there anymore! Her new house is different, altogether beautiful. The foundation is strong, built solely on the rock. The windows are large, the vision is crystal clear, and the Son comes shining brightly through. The doors are open; the house is inviting. The bread is plentiful, and the water is overflowing. This new house is her home. She finally unpacked, and she's never moving out!

Have a Radiant Day!

TODAY'S RADIANT REVELATION:

_____

_____

_____

_____

_____

_____

_____

_____

_____

_____

_____

_____

_____

_____

_____

_____

_____

_____

_____

_____

_____

_____

Day 3

Shame Has to Go

◆

To grant those who mourn in Zion, Giving them a garland instead of ashes, The oil of gladness instead of mourning, The mantle of praise instead of a spirit of fainting. So they will be called oaks of righteousness. The planting of the Lord, that he may be glorified.

Isaiah 61:3

◆

Shame, oh how I hate her! She suspends you to the darkest place in time and relentlessly attempts to keep you there. She paralyzes progress, she's purgatory to purpose. She's envious of your future so she chains you to your past. She imprisons your mind and shackles your soul. She knows you well, she's you!

Sit her down and tell her about the good news. Tell her that shame has no power in the presence of the good news. Inform her that the good news sets the captives free, that it's a consuming fire and burns condemnation to the ground. Declare that the good news restores and redeems!

Inform her that shame and redemption make horrible roommates. Give her the power to choose who stays!

Have a Radiant Day!

TODAY'S RADIANT REVELATION:

Day 4

Crave the Creator

◆

Like newborn babies, long for the pure milk of the word, so
that by it you may grow in respect to salvation, if you have
tasted the kindness of the Lord.

1 Peter 2:2-3

◆

Any woman that has ever breastfed understands how difficult it is to wean her baby. The baby may start off breastfeeding hesitantly, but once the little one latches on, they're completely attached and addicted to their mother's milk. So much so, that it becomes almost impossible to feed a breastfed baby ANYTHING else! Why? Because they have tasted the SINCERE milk and as a result, their palates have been trained to spot an imposter. The same should hold true for our spiritual appetites. The scripture tells us that in these last days, we will have an appetite for false doctrine, spiritually fake food that feels good going down, but offers no eternal substance. We'll feast on empty calories, yearning to be filled with joy, only to be left feeling deprived time and time again. We'll binge on processed, genetically modified, artificial catechisms that cannot and will not sustain us during the battle ahead of us. The time is up for spiritually malnourished women! Taste the sincere milk of the Word of Elohim, feed on sound doctrine, and strengthen your spiritual muscles!

Have a Radiant Day!

Randi Meacham

_____

_____

_____

_____

_____

_____

_____

_____

_____

_____

_____

_____

_____

_____

_____

_____

_____

_____

_____

_____

_____

_____

Day 5

Fully Armored

◆

Put on the full armor of God, so that you will be able
to stand firm against the schemes of the devil.

Ephesians 6:11

◆

If someone informed you that you had an archenemy, what would you do? If you knew that he was hostile towards you, had sheer hatred for you, and loathed everything about you, how would you respond? And then, what if you learned that this enemy hated your seed? And that he was on a mission to antagonize, avert, and abort everything that you have given or will give birth to. How would you respond? Would you stand by idly and watch him destroy everything that you love OR would you don your full armor and prepare to fight?

Well, my sister, you've been warned! You do have an enemy, and he has been at enmity with you and your seed since the beginning of time. He's after the seed of your faith, the seed of your family, and the seed of your future! He's your enemy so don't be deceived. He's on a mission to kill everything that the Father has planted within you. So put on your full armor, get in the spiritual arena, and fight!

Have a Radiant Day!

TODAY'S RADIANT REVELATION:

_____

_____

_____

_____

_____

_____

_____

_____

_____

_____

_____

_____

_____

_____

_____

_____

_____

_____

_____

_____

_____

_____

Day 6

Claim Your Crown

◆

Giving thanks to the Father, who has qualified us to
share in the inheritance of the saints in Light.

Colossians 1:12

◆

Imagine going on a shopping spree where money was not an object. Everything that your heart desires is yours for the taking. A fabulous purse, gorgeous pair of shoes, and that sassy outfit that you've been eyeing forever...ALL PAID FOR! Then imagine, you become distracted and carelessly walk out of the boutique without your bags, only to return to find that they're gone. A thief has stolen your possessions! The anger and disappointment would be real! How much more disappointing is it when we carelessly allow the prince of thieves to steal our eternal treasure? The Messiah paid it all! Salvation is yours, peace is yours, joy is yours, healing is yours, deliverance is yours. Don't forfeit your future by becoming distracted. The enemy wants to steal your inheritance. Grasp your gifts, cling to your calling, claim your crown!

Have a Radiant Day!

TODAY'S RADIANT REVELATION:

_____

_____

_____

_____

_____

_____

_____

_____

_____

_____

_____

_____

_____

_____

_____

_____

_____

_____

_____

Day 7

Stand Up, Rise Up, Grow Up!

◆

When I was a child, I used to speak like a child, think like a child, reason like a child; when I became a man, I did away with childish things.

1 Corinthians 13:11

◆

The kingdom of heaven is at hand! The Most High is enlisting an army of wise women who aren't silly or easily swayed by evil desires. He's seeking women who are mission minded and vision focused. Those who have no need for constant validation but find their identity in Christ. He's seeking wise women! He's seeking strong women, women who have graduated from the school of hard knocks and have earned their degrees in life. He's seeking those who have strategically studied their failures and refuse to repeat the same courses OVER and OVER and OVER again. He's seeking those who are equipped to teach others rather than constantly desiring to be taught, ever learning but never coming to the knowledge of truth. The time is now. Stand up, rise up, and grow up!

Have a Radiant Day!

TODAY'S RADIANT REVELATION:

_____

_____

_____

_____

_____

_____

_____

_____

_____

_____

_____

_____

_____

_____

_____

_____

_____

_____

_____

_____

_____

_____

Day 8

The Intentional Life

◆

Strength and dignity are her clothing,

And she smiles at the future.

She opens her mouth in wisdom,

And the teaching of kindness is on her tongue.

She looks well to the ways of her household,

And does not eat the bread of idleness.

Her children rise up and bless her;

Her husband also, and he praises her, saying:

"Many daughters have done nobly,

But you excel them all."

Charm is deceitful and beauty is vain,

But a woman who fears the Lord, she shall be praised.

Give her the product of her hands,

And let her works praise her in the gates.

Proverbs 31:25-31

◆

A wise woman is a deliberate woman. When she speaks, she has something to say. She's intentional and instinctual, focused and fearless. She's guarded, yet graceful. Elohim is her foundation and the rock that keeps her grounded. She cannot, she will not be moved. She prays before she proceeds. She protects what's hers and rejects what's not. She's on a mission to fulfill the great commission. Her faith is her pulpit, her character is her sermon, and her life is her testimony. Live intentionally!

Have a Radiant Day!

TODAY'S RADIANT REVELATION:

Day 9

Taste and See

◆

*"You are the light of the world. A city set on a hill cannot be hidden;
nor does anyone light a lamp and put it under a basket, but on the
lampstand, and it gives light to all who are in the house. Let your
light shine before men in such a way that they may see your good
works, and glorify your Father who is in heaven."*

Matthew 5:14-16

◆

Anyone who has ever been on a diet knows exactly how it feels to be
ravishingly hungry. You deprive yourself of food for a period of time,
and when your willpower fails, you devour everything in sight. You
feast on anything just to fulfill the void of hunger. The same holds
true for our spiritual appetites. When we choose not to feast on the
word of Elohim, we become spiritually deprived. We fail to
understand our identity in Christ and begin to relish the images of this
world, scavenging for fulfillment. Our bodies become weak, and
instead of treating it as the temple that Elohim created it to be, we
seek to quench our thirst with ungodly or unhealthy relationships.

29

True fulfillment can ONLY be found in a relationship with the Father. Taste and see that the He is good and never hunger or thirst again!

Have a Radiant Day!

TODAY'S RADIANT REVELATION:

_____

_____

_____

_____

_____

_____

_____

_____

_____

_____

_____

_____

_____

_____

_____

_____

_____

_____

_____

_____

_____

_____

_____

_____

Day 10

Woman of Valor

◆

An excellent wife, who can find? For her worth is far above jewels.

Proverbs 31:10

◆

What does it mean to be a virtuous woman? Having high moral standards? Yes! But a virtuous woman is so much more. Webster's definition is abstract and is defined as having or displaying high moral standards (righteous, good, pure, etc.). But *chayil* is the Hebrew word for virtuous and is much more instructional! A mandate for how to BE! *Chayil* in Hebrew is defined as having strength and is often used in conjunction with words such as mighty, warrior, valiant, substance, and power. The *chayil* woman is not a weak or needy woman. She is described in Proverbs 31, as a woman of strength, courage, and ingenuity! She's intelligent and instinctual. She's a fighter and a force to be reckoned with. She's idealistic, not idle. She's a seer and not just eye candy. She knows who she is and what she's called to do. She doesn't follow the crowd because the narrow gate is her compass. She's completely feminine and completely fierce. Be *chayil*!

Have a Radiant Day!

Randi Meacham

TODAY'S RADIANT REVELATION:

_____

_____

_____

_____

_____

_____

_____

_____

_____

_____

_____

_____

_____

_____

_____

_____

_____

_____

_____

_____

_____

Day 11

Abba's Girl

◆

He predestined us to adoption as sons through Jesus Christ to Himself, according to the kind intention of his will, to the praise of the glory of His grace, which He freely bestowed on us in the Beloved.

Ephesians 1:5-6

◆

She's a daddy's girl! She has always been keenly aware of this for as long as she could remember. He was the core of her existence, he validated her. He placed her on a pedestal so high, that anyone who dared to touch her had to be reaching for the stars themselves. She was his beautiful princess, and he was her knight in shining armor. She soared like an eagle because to her, he was the moon, the sun, and the wind beneath her wings. Yes, she has always been a daddy's girl. Unfortunately, daddy turned out to be only a figment of her imagination. The contradiction of her inner princess and reality rendered her helpless against the attack of the enemy. Daddy wasn't sitting on the porch with the proverbial "shotgun" which left the door open for thieves to break in to kill, steal, and destroy.

Oh, but now! She has a kinsman redeemer, and He has adopted her into his family. He calls her his own. He sticks closer to her than a brother. He laid down his life for her. He has prepared a place for her. He wraps her in the cradle of His arms. He's a strong tower that protects her. The enemy came to kill, steal, and destroy; but her Father is sitting on the throne so that she may have life and have it more abundantly. Yes! She is a Daddy's girl, and He's not just her knight in shining armor, He's her King of Kings! If you haven't been adopted, you too can become a part of the family. No blood test required, it has already been shed for you on Calvary.

Have a Radiant Day!

TODAY'S RADIANT REVELATION:

_____

_____

_____

_____

_____

_____

_____

_____

_____

_____

_____

_____

_____

_____

_____

_____

_____

_____

_____

_____

_____

_____

_____

Day 12

Kingdom Authority

◆

But you are a chosen race, a royal priesthood, a holy nation, a people for God's own possession, so that you may proclaim the excellencies of Him who has called you out of darkness into His marvelous light;

1 Peter 2:9

◆

How radiant is the woman who walks in the kingdom's authority! There's an awakening in the Spirit. Her vision is clear; she's keenly aware of her purpose. She walks intentionally and unapologetically on the journey to claim her inheritance. She believes who Elohim says that she is, and she carries her sword to victoriously cast down the lies of the thief who comes to steal her joy. Her mission is to live the abundant life. She understands that it is hers for the taking. She boldly proclaims the good news of her deliverer. She rejoices in her healing. Depression can't withstand the radiance of her joy. Darkness has no authority in the brilliance of her light. Death has no sting in the sparkle of her life. You're the daughter of the King, adjust your crown and reign victoriously.

Have a Radiant Day!

Randi Meacham

TODAY'S RADIANT REVELATION:

Day 13

Free to Forgive

◆

For if you forgive others for their transgressions, your heavenly Father will also forgive you. But if you do not forgive others, then your Father will not forgive your transgressions.

Matthew 6:14-15

◆

How do you forgive someone when the pain is so deep within that not even you can locate all of its remnants? How can you release someone from the prison of condemnation when you feel that they've never even served their sentence? How do you emancipate yourself from the guilt of your past when the clothing of shame is all that you have hanging in your closet?

Many of us live defeated lives because we've allowed unforgiveness to take up residence in our hearts. Instead of casting our cares upon the one who cares for us, we load them up and carry them on the backs of our souls. The heaviness renders us stranded in time, shipwrecked to a place that forfeits our ability to sail away freely from the hurt. Maybe he left you to carry the load of raising the kids on your own, FORGIVE. Maybe your mother or father wasn't there for you, FORGIVE. Maybe you were used and abused, FORGIVE. Maybe you were the offender, FORGIVE yourself! The power of the Holy Spirit dwells within us, and just as the Messiah offers the gift of forgiveness, He commands, not suggests, that we forgive both ourselves and those who have sinned against us as well. You will never live the victorious life that Elohim has prepared for you until you release everything and everyone that has kept you bound. Free others that you may be free!

Have a Radiant Day!

TODAY'S RADIANT REVELATION:

_____
_____
_____
_____
_____
_____
_____
_____
_____
_____
_____
_____
_____
_____
_____
_____
_____
_____
_____
_____
_____
_____
_____
_____
_____

Day 14

More Than Enough

◆

She is more precious than jewels;

And nothing you desire compares with her.

Long life is in her right hand;

In her left hand are riches and honor.

Her ways are pleasant ways

And all her paths are peace.

She is a tree of life to those who take hold of her,

And happy are all who hold her fast.

Proverbs 3:15-18

◆

What words have been spoken over your life? Are they utterances of affirmation? Do they declare that you're fearfully and wonderfully made? Are they whispers of the Song of Solomon that proclaim, "You are altogether beautiful and that there is no flaw in you?"

Or have you allowed the lie of the enemy to speak into your spirit? Has he told you that you're not smart enough or attractive enough or thin enough or enough? If so declare..."I am enough! My identity lies solely in The Most High. Not in man, not in my past, not in the world's definition of beauty."

Shout out loud, "I was created in the image of Elohim; He calls me His own." Testify that even when I dwelled in the pit of ugliness, Elohim loved me so much that He sent His Son to redeem me! Reclaim your identity in eternity.

Have a Radiant Day!

Randi Meacham

Day 15

Get Up!

◆

But Peter sent them all out and knelt down and prayed, and turning to the body, he said, "Tabitha, arise." And she opened her eyes, and when she saw Peter, she sat up. And he gave her his hand and raised her up; and calling the saints and widows, he presented her alive. It became known all over Joppa, and many believed in the Lord.

Acts 9:40-42

◆

What would happen if you just got up? If you decided today, that you would no longer allow the grave of guilt to keep you bound or the casket of condemnation to hold you captive? If you just got up, whose life could you change? You will never lift others if you keep lying down. Open your eyes and arise! Your family and friends are waiting, your future is waiting, the kingdom is waiting... GET UP!

Have a Radiant Day!

TODAY'S RADIANT REVELATION:

_____

_____

_____

_____

_____

_____

_____

_____

_____

_____

_____

_____

_____

_____

_____

_____

_____

_____

_____

_____

_____

Day 16

The Hand That Rocks the Cradle

◆

Older women likewise are to be reverent in their behavior, not
malicious gossips nor enslaved to much wine, teaching what is
good, so that they may encourage the young women to love
their husbands, to love their children, to be sensible, pure,
workers at home, kind, being subject to their own husbands, so
that the word of God will not be dishonored.

Titus 2:3-5

◆

The hand that rocks the cradle rules the world, yet when those hands are weak and wounded, the cradle is left unattended and rendered defenseless against the enemies attack. Could it be that our world is sick because women are transferring generational curses? Women that truly understand who they are, reflect the confidence of being fearfully and wonderfully made. This woman does not spread the infection of insecurity to the young women in her life. She serves as a role model, keenly aware of her worth, and her decisions reflect the same. When a woman walks in the authority of their royal priesthood, no longer does she transmit the epidemic of ego to the young men in her life. She is a reflection of strength and courage, and as a result, the young men under her tutelage seek the same strength in the women that they choose. He's secure enough to choose a wife who walks by his side and not in his shadow.

The time is now! Be discharged from the hospital of hopelessness; be delivered from the disease of dysfunction. Walk boldly in your healing so that through you, your daughters and sons, granddaughters and grandsons, family and friends, our communities, and this world may be healed as well.

Have a Radiant Day!

TODAY'S RADIANT REVELATION:

_____

_____

_____

_____

_____

_____

_____

_____

_____

_____

_____

_____

_____

_____

_____

_____

_____

_____

_____

_____

_____

_____

Day 17

Be Healed

◆

And He said to her, "Daughter, your
faith has made you well; go in peace and
be healed of your affliction."

Mark 5:34

◆

She suffered for twelve years until she decided, *No more*! No longer would she carry the weight of her issue. She decided to walk by faith, on a journey to receive her healing. The doctors could not heal her, her family could not ease the pain, and the community had cast her aside. Her issue could only be healed by the touch of the Messiah. Courageously, she pressed through the crowd. She chose to risk it all for His touch. Are you sick from the circumstances of life? Have you been diagnosed with the disease of defeat, a hemorrhage of hate, or a broken heart? Like the woman with the issue of blood, you must fight for your healing and walk boldly by faith to receive it... There's healing power in the Messiah. Healing is a choice; choose to receive it or the "issue is you."

Have a Radiant Day!

TODAY'S RADIANT REVELATION:

_____
_____
_____
_____
_____
_____
_____
_____
_____
_____
_____
_____
_____
_____
_____
_____
_____
_____
_____
_____

Day 18

No Longer Condemned

◆

For I am convinced that neither death, nor life, nor angels, nor principalities, nor things present, nor things to come, nor powers, nor height, nor depth, nor any other created thing, will be able to separate us from the love of God, which is in Christ Jesus our Lord.

Romans 8:38-39

◆

Condemnation is a cancer! It begins in your mind and infects every area of your life. It spreads to your eyes, and you begin to see yourself as your mistakes rather than the woman that Elohim created you to be. It travels to your lips, and you begin to speak word curses over your life and the lives of your loved ones. It permeates in your heart and renders you to a state of paralysis, incapable of loving or receiving love. Be encouraged, beautiful! Elohim loves you, and there is NOTHING that can separate you from His love. Satan wants to keep you bound, but Christ is the cure to set you free.

Have a Radiant Day!

TODAY'S RADIANT REVELATION:

_____

_____

_____

_____

_____

_____

_____

_____

_____

_____

_____

_____

_____

_____

_____

_____

_____

_____

_____

_____

_____

_____

Day 19

Speak Life

◆

She opens her mouth in wisdom,
And the teaching of kindness is on her tongue.

Proverbs 31:26

◆

Are you speaking life? Are you declaring the praises of Him who called you out of darkness into the marvelous light? Words have power! Negativity breeds negativity. One word has the power to produce life or spawn death! Speak affirmations of strength and courage? Take back what the enemy has stolen through the words that you've spoken over your life or the lives of your loved ones. Resurrect that which was killed by your words. Declare hope, proclaim freedom, and speak life!

Have a Radiant Day!

TODAY'S RADIANT REVELATION:

_____

_____

_____

_____

_____

_____

_____

_____

_____

_____

_____

_____

_____

_____

_____

_____

_____

_____

_____

_____

_____

_____

_____

Day 20

Never Thirst Again

◆

From that city many of the Samaritans believed in Him
because of the word of the woman who testified, "He
told me all the things that I have done."

John 4:39

◆

She came from the wrong side of the tracks. Poor in spirit and thirsting for validation, she sought it out in ungodly relationships. First time empty, second time broken, third time hurt, fourth time disappointed, fifth time confused, sixth time numb! BUT THEN, she met a man who knew her and everything that she had done, and despite her sin, He quenched her dying thirst with living water that she never thirsted again.

Like the Samaritan woman, many of us seek validation in people, possessions, and even ungodly relationships. However until we encounter the spring of water welling up to eternal life, we will never truly be fulfilled. The woman at the well accepted the overflowing gift of Christ, and because of her willingness to share her testimony, others were delivered as well. Drink from the well and share what you've received. We are living in a desert with people thirsting for truth!

Have a Radiant Day!

Randi Meacham

TODAY'S RADIANT REVELATION:

_____

_____

_____

_____

_____

_____

_____

_____

_____

_____

_____

_____

_____

_____

_____

_____

_____

_____

_____

_____

_____

_____

Day 21

Mission Minded, Vision Focused

◆

*These twelve Jesus sent out after instructing them: "Do not go
in the way of the Gentiles, and do not enter any city of the
Samaritans; but rather go to the lost sheep of the house of
Israel. And as you go, preach, saying, 'The kingdom of heaven
is at hand.' Heal the sick, raise the dead, cleanse the lepers,
cast out demons. Freely you received, freely give.*

Matthew 10:5-8

◆

There can be no intentional living without strategic, intentional relationships. How amazing it is that Christ lived on earth for only thirty-three years and of those thirty-three years, twenty-one of those were in ministry. The Messiah was strategic in His associations because He was keenly aware of His mission. The souls of a lost and dying world were at hand; eternity was at stake. Time was of the essence and could not be spent on the inconsequential things of this world. The gospel had to be preached, the sick had to be healed, and the hungry had to be fed. Christ had to die for our sins, be buried, and resurrected. He chose the twelve disciples to assist him in carrying out this mission, and although they were not perfect, He utilized both their strengths and weaknesses to manifest the perfect plan. What has the Most High called you to do? Are the people in your life helping or hindering that calling? Never confuse reason relationships with season relationships or season relationships with lifetime relationships. When seasons collide, storms arise and the mission loses momentum. Don't squander the life that Elohim has blessed you with on relationships that are not beneficial to His plan. Your relationships either help or hinder the mission, be mission minded and vision focused.

Have a Radiant Day!

TODAY'S RADIANT REVELATION:

_____

_____

_____

_____

_____

_____

_____

_____

_____

_____

_____

_____

_____

_____

_____

_____

_____

_____

_____

_____

_____

_____

Randi Meacham

Day 22

Who Are You?

◆

The nations will see your righteousness,

And all kings your glory;

And you will be called by a new name

Which the mouth of the Lord will designate.

You will also be a crown of beauty in the hand of the Lord,

And a royal diadem in the hand of your God.

It will no longer be said to you, "Forsaken,"

Nor to your land will it any longer be said,

"Desolate";

But you will be called, "My delight is in her,"

And your land, "Married";

For the Lord delights in you,

And to Him your land will be married.

For as a young man marries a virgin,

So your sons will marry you;

And as the bridegroom rejoices over the bride,

So your God will rejoice over you.

Isaiah 62:2-5

Who do you think you are? Are you a mountain mover or a desert dweller?

The children of Israel wandered aimlessly in the desert for forty years because they failed to comprehend the magnitude of their greatness. They walked through the Red Sea, yet lacked the courage to stand on solid ground; they ate manna rained down from heaven, but were not filled with faith; they drank water turned to wine, but allowed unbelief to quench their spirit. Their lack of faith rendered them blind to the leadership of Moses and deaf to the voice of Elohim. They relied on their familiar state of bondage. Their physical chains were broken, but they remained mentally imprisoned. Royal by race, slaves in stature.

Are the shadows of your past blinding you from the radiance of your future?

Like many of us, the children of Israel allowed their years of slavery to keep them in a stagnant state. They had been told of their greatness; they had even witnessed miracles; however, they allowed the circumstances of their past to alter the trajectory of their future. Don't allow Satan to whisper the tingling symbols of chains in your spirit. Hear the sound of freedom, be strategic in your pursuit of promise, and walk boldly into the promised land!

Have a Radiant Day!

TODAY'S RADIANT REVELATION:

_____

_____

_____

_____

_____

_____

_____

_____

_____

_____

_____

_____

_____

_____

_____

_____

_____

_____

_____

_____

_____

_____

_____

_____

_____

Day 23

Rise Up!

◆

Do this, knowing the time, that it is already the hour for you to awaken from sleep; for now salvation is nearer to us that when we believed. The night is almost gone, and the day is near. Therefore let us lay aside the deeds of darkness and put on the armor of light. Let us behave properly as in the day, not in carousing and drunkenness, not in sexual promiscuity and sensuality, not in strife and jealousy. But put on the Lord Jesus Christ, and make no provision for the flesh in regard to its lusts.

Romans 13:11-14

◆

Arise and shine! Arise from the slumber of the status quo. Stir up the spirit that you've allowed to lie dormant for so long. Do what sets your soul on fire! Spark the kindling flame! Spread the wildfire! Share the good news! Give of your time, your talents, and your resources!

The birthing pain of Christ's return is growing louder. Are you alert? Can you hear it? Sound the alarm! Be the alarm! Wake up! No time to sleep, the kingdom of heaven is at hand! Stop insulting your soul!

Have a Radiant Day!

TODAY'S RADIANT REVELATION:

_____

_____

_____

_____

_____

_____

_____

_____

_____

_____

_____

_____

_____

_____

_____

_____

_____

_____

_____

_____

_____

_____

_____

_____

_____

Day 24

Dignity Is Her Favorite Brand

◆

Strength and dignity are her clothing,

And she smiles at the future.

She opens her mouth in wisdom,

And the teaching of kindness is on her tongue.

Proverbs 31:25-26

◆

There's nothing more beautiful than a confident woman. Not the confidence that is derived from superficial beauty or outward adornment, no, it's the kind of beauty that can only be attained by living. It's the scars of women who have been beaten down by the circumstances of life, but were strong enough to dust themselves off and resume the fight. It's the diamonds of disappointment, the rubies of rejection, and the pearls of peril. It's the beauty that radiates in darkness and defeats despair, of a virtuous woman. Dignity is her favorite brand, and she wears it well! She laughs without fear of the future because she's confident in her destination.

Be her, teach your daughters to become her, and your sons to seek her… This world needs more warriors like her!

Have a Radiant Day!

TODAY'S RADIANT REVELATION:

Day 25

Healed, Filled, Redeemed, and Restored

◆

I will stand on my guard post
And station myself on the rampart;
And I will keep watch to see what He will speak to me,
And how I may reply when I am reproved.

Habakkuk 2:1

◆

The woman with the issue wanted to be healed,

The woman at the well wanted to be filled.

Ruth just wanted to belong,

Deborah just wanted to right the wrongs.

Esther was the orphan who became a queen,

She accepted the call and her people were redeemed.

And though none of these women sought a position,

They all were in the perfect position to be healed, filled, redeemed, and restored.

Have a Radiant Day!

TODAY'S RADIANT REVELATION:

Day 26

The Potter Wants to Put You Back Together

◆

Heal me, O Lord, and I will be healed;

Save me and I will be saved,

For You are my praise.

Jeremiah 17:14

◆

Are you living a shattered life?

Have you been crushed by your past? Are the fragments of your pain cutting the people that you love? Are you broken and brittle, difficult to touch? You'll never be complete until the Father makes you whole. Allow the Potter to put your broken pieces back together again.

Have a Radiant Day!

TODAY'S RADIANT REVELATION:

_____

_____

_____

_____

_____

_____

_____

_____

_____

_____

_____

_____

_____

_____

_____

_____

_____

_____

_____

_____

_____

_____

_____

Day 27

He Can Use Your Kind

◆

"For this reason I say to you, her sins,
which are many, have been forgiven, for
she loved much; but he who is forgiven
little, loves little."
Luke 7:47

◆

No longer was she bound by the shame that had silenced her for so long. Not willing to wait her turn, she pressed through the crowd, ignoring the judgmental demands of the theologically correct. She anointed her Savior with all that she had, as He had forgiven her for all that she had done. She opened her heart and found her voice.

If Elohim has called you to do a work, listen! Don't be silenced by anyone who tells you that it's not your season or that your sin is too great! The woman heard the Master's call and pressed through the crowd. And because of her bold, intentional, unapologetic faith, she was healed!

Ask Elohim to place people in your life that will cultivate your strengths and undergird your weaknesses. He can use "your kind" for His glory. Don't allow others to judge your story by the chapter they walked in on. They don't know the cost!

Have a Radiant Day!

TODAY'S RADIANT REVELATION:

_____

_____

_____

_____

_____

_____

_____

_____

_____

_____

_____

_____

_____

_____

_____

_____

_____

_____

_____

_____

_____

_____

_____

_____

_____

Day 28

Choose Life

◆

The thief comes only to steal and kill and
destroy; I came that they may have life,
and have it abundantly.

John 10:10

◆

A broken woman fights, a healed woman defends.

A broken woman destroys, a healed woman mends.

A broken woman hates, a healed woman forgives.

A broken woman is dying within, a healed woman lives.

Have a Radiant Day!

TODAY'S RADIANT REVELATION:

_____

_____

_____

_____

_____

_____

_____

_____

_____

_____

_____

_____

_____

_____

_____

_____

_____

_____

_____

_____

_____

Day 29

On Eagles' Wings

◆

Yet those who wait for the Lord
Will gain new strength;
They will mount up with wings like eagles,
They will run and not get tired,
They will walk and not become weary.

Isaiah 40:31

◆

So often we pray that Elohim will deliver or shield us from the difficulties in life. We pray for strength and endurance, and yet we seek to forfeit the training that produces it. When a mother bird lays her egg, instead of utilizing the strength of her beak to release the baby bird from the captivity of its shell, she sits on it and patiently waits. Just when the baby bird has reached the age of maturity, she steps aside, never far away, and witnesses her miracle breaking free. Freedom is on the horizon, yet the struggle has just begun. The baby bird struggles to release itself from the hard shell that has kept it bound; it presses through the cracks of captivity. The struggle produces life! Without the struggle, the baby bird's wings would not strengthened; without the pressing, it's lung capacity would not be tested. Without strong wings, a bird never flies; without strong lungs, the eagle never soars!!! Allow Elohim to strengthen your wings... Eagles fly high!

Have a Radiant Day!

TODAY'S RADIANT REVELATION:

Day 30

Restorer of the Breach

◆

"And the Lord will continually guide you,
And satisfy your desire in scorched places,
And give strength to your bones;
And you will be like a watered garden,
And like a spring of water whose waters do not fail.
Those from among you will rebuild the ancient ruins;
You will raise up the age-old foundations;
And you will be called the repairer of the breach,
The restorer of the streets in which to dwell."

Isaiah 58:11-12

◆

Is there a breach in your foundation? Do you find yourself continuously patching up the proverbial leaky holes in your life only to discover yet another leak? Quite often, we attempt to fight battles that were waged against and lost by generations before us. We inherit and pass on these soul defects, because instead of repairing the problem, we become immune to the dripping. We place pots in the center of our souls and allow the holes to grow in size. We become oblivious to the dark places in our spirits and afford opportunities for them to manifest themselves in other areas. Christ came to set the captives free. He laid down His life to restore that which was lost; He came to repair our leaky souls so that we may reclaim all that was lost in the flood. Climb aboard the ark of deliverance and don your life jacket of grace. Repair the leaks in your life and gift the next generation with restoration.

Have a Radiant Day!

TODAY'S RADIANT REVELATION:

_____

_____

_____

_____

_____

_____

_____

_____

_____

_____

_____

_____

_____

_____

_____

_____

_____

_____

_____

_____

_____

_____

Day 31

A Tapestry of Testimonies

◆

And we know that God causes all things to work
together for good to those who love God, to those who
are called according to His purpose.

Romans 8:28

◆

Your life is a beautiful montage... a carefully constructed tapestry of testimonies. The good, the bad, and the ugly are all designed to mold you into the image of the Most High. Be encouraged, forge ahead in faith, and know that when Elohim gets through with you, you will come forth as pure gold.

Have a Radiant Day!

A 40-Day Journal of Radiant Revelations

TODAY'S RADIANT REVELATION:

_____
_____
_____
_____
_____
_____
_____
_____
_____
_____
_____
_____
_____
_____
_____
_____
_____
_____
_____
_____

Day 32

Your Life Is A Song

◆

He put a new song in my mouth, a song of praise to our God;

Many will see and fear

And will trust in the Lord.

Psalm 40:3

◆

Your life is a song. Are the lyrics a joyful chorus line? Is it a beautiful compilation of strength and victory? Is there a rhythmic cadence that encourages the listener to dance in freedom? Or do the symbols of your life pierce the soul of those who listen to the screeching sounds of despair and defeat? Sing a new song of praise and make a joyful noise unto Elohim. Serenade the world with a glorious melody of the good news of our Savior!

Have a Radiant Day!

TODAY'S RADIANT REVELATION:

_____

_____

_____

_____

_____

_____

_____

_____

_____

_____

_____

_____

_____

_____

_____

_____

_____

_____

_____

_____

_____

_____

_____

Day 33

Break Every Chain

◆

It is for freedom that Christ set us free; therefore keep standing firm and do not be subject again to a yoke of slavery.

Galatians 5:1

◆

Juneteenth is a holiday widely celebrated. This holiday commemorates the freeing of enslaved Africans in the state of Texas on June 19, 1865, three years after the Emancipation Proclamation. Because of Texas' geographical location, this good news was easily withheld from those who were enslaved, thus rendering them to a state of bondage well past their emancipation.

The Messiah's death and resurrection emancipated us from the penalty of sin. How many years past your emancipation have you continued to walk in bondage, cut off from the good news, enslaved to sin and fear? What plantation has the Most High delivered you from that you keep returning back to? Escape from the oppression of your past, release the shackles of shame, proclaim your emancipation. Who the Son sets free is free indeed!

TODAY'S RADIANT REVELATION:

_____

_____

_____

_____

_____

_____

_____

_____

_____

_____

_____

_____

_____

_____

_____

_____

_____

_____

Day 34

Choose Healing

◆

Heal me, O Lord, and I will be healed;

Save me and I will be saved,

For You are my praise.

Jeremiah 17:14

◆

Imagine being diagnosed with a communicable disease. You find out that not only are you infected, but you are at risk of infecting everyone around you as well. And then you meet with your physician to receive the good news that there is a cure. "Take this medication as prescribed," the doctor explains, "and you will be cured!" You ponder over your options and haphazardly choose not to take the medication. How irresponsible would that be? Through this decision, you effectively resolve not only to remain ill, but to also risk the well-being of everyone around you. Well, we do this when we choose not to be healed of our brokenness. We choose to remain infected with insecurities, diseased with dysfunction, and contaminated with condemnation. We pass on this vicious viral cycle from one generation to the next. Healing is yours! Accept the prescription of the Great Physician and be healed! Do it for yourself, do it for your family, and do it for the kingdom!

Have a Radiant Day!

TODAY'S RADIANT REVELATION:

_____
_____
_____
_____
_____
_____
_____
_____
_____
_____
_____
_____
_____
_____
_____
_____
_____
_____
_____
_____
_____
_____
_____
_____

Day 35

The Power of Women

◆

"Most blessed of women is Jael,
The wife of Heber the Kenite;
Most blessed is she of women in the tent.
He asked for water and she gave him milk.
In a magnificent bowl she brought him curds.
She reached out her hand for a tent peg,
And her right hand for the workman's hammer.
Then she struck Sisera, she smashed his head;
And she shattered and pierced his temple.
Between her feet he bowed, he fell, he lay;
Between her feet he bowed, he fell;
Where he bowed, there he fell dead."
Judges 5:24-27

◆

We're living in a time very reminiscent to the days of the book of Judges. Like the children of Israel, we've abandoned the road that leads to righteousness and detoured down the path that leads to destruction. Village life has ceased to exist because we've taken up residence on the island of ME!

Will you rise up like Deborah? Like Jael, will you destroy the enemy with one shattering blow? If we would just rise up, the enemy would sink and fall dead at our feet! Never underestimate the power of women.

Have a Radiant Day!

TODAY'S RADIANT REVELATION:

_____

_____

_____

_____

_____

_____

_____

_____

_____

_____

_____

_____

_____

_____

_____

_____

_____

_____

_____

_____

_____

_____

Day 36

Give Birth

◆

"And blessed is she who has believed that there would be a fulfillment

of what had been spoken to her by the Lord."

And Mary said:

"My soul exalts the Lord,

And my spirit has rejoiced in God my Savior.

For he has had regard for the humble state of His bondslave;

For behold, from this time on all generations will count me blessed.

For the Mighty One has done great things for me;

And holy is his name.

And His mercy is upon generation after generation

Toward those who fear him."

Luke 1:45-50

◆

What is Elohim birthing in you? Is there a calling upon your life that you feel unworthy to answer? Are there gifts lying dormant within you, waiting to manifest themselves? Maybe it's the all important salvation of your soul? Has the enemy convinced you that your past or your present or even your future renders you unworthy of this eternal gift? The enemy desires to keep you in bondage. Elohim desires to set you free! Mary's belief birthed the Savior; what will your belief birth? If Elohim said it, that settles it! Stand boldly on His promises and claim your inheritance.

Have a Radiant Day!

Randi Meacham

Day 37

Keep Standing!

◆

Therefore, take up the full armor of God,
so that you will be able to resist in the
evil day, and having done everything, to
stand firm.
Ephesians 6:13

◆

Distraction is one of the enemy's craftiest schemes. He distracts us with worry, he distracts us with fear, and he distracts us with doubt. He knows that if he can catch us off balance, he can infiltrate our thoughts, and if he infiltrates our thoughts, he can strangulate our prayers, and if he strangulates our prayers, he can suffocate our purpose. It may feel uncomfortable; it may even hurt, but tighten up those sandals of peace and having done all things to stand, stand some more!

Have a Radiant Day!

TODAY'S RADIANT REVELATION:

Day 38

Don't Turn Back

◆

But Ruth said, "Do not urge me to leave you or turn back from following you; for where you go, I will go, and where you lodge, I will lodge. Your people shall be my people, and your God, my God."

Ruth 1:16

◆

Ruth made a decision that changed the trajectory of her future. She chose not to turn back! She chose not to turn back to the people of her past. She chose not to turn back to the places of her past. She chose not to turn back to the pain of her past. She decided to go! Make up your mind to move forward in faith and just go!

Have a Radiant Day!

Randi Meacham

TODAY'S RADIANT REVELATION:

Day 39

No Place Like Home

◆

For here we do not have a lasting city, but we are
seeking the city which is to come.

Hebrews 13:14

◆

There's no place like home! It doesn't matter how luxurious the décor or delicious the food or gracious the host. There is nothing more comforting than relaxing in your own space with the things that you treasure surrounding you and the people that you love embracing you. Utopia is the place where all is right with your world even when everything in the world around you seems to be going wrong. At home, there's joy, there's peace, there's refuge.

But where is your home?

Have you laid your foundation on the promises of this world? Where moth and rust corrupt? Have you stored treasures where thieves break in and steal? Have you unpacked your eternal promises in a false sense of security closet? Have you become so comfortable and complacent with your temporary residence that you've failed to prepare for your forever home? Don't be deceived by the schemes of the enemy; this world is not your home! Build your hopes on things eternal and prepare for relocation to the indestructible mansion in paradise.

Have a Radiant Day!

TODAY'S RADIANT REVELATION:

_____

_____

_____

_____

_____

_____

_____

_____

_____

_____

_____

_____

_____

_____

_____

_____

_____

_____

_____

_____

_____

_____

_____

_____

_____

_____

_____

Day 40

Free Indeed

◆

So if the Son makes you free, you will be free indeed.

John 8:36

◆

The prison shuffle is a term that describes the gait of an incarcerated individual. This is an unmistakable posture. Legs bound together; head hung low; short, quick steps. This stride results from years of incarceration. Prisoners are often required to wear chains around their ankles, and after functioning for years in a state of bondage, this stride becomes automatic. After their debt to society has been paid, freedom ensues. No longer bound by chains, they're capable of standing tall, and yet the shuffle remains. Free from the chains, they are still shackled in the mind.

Are you treading down the path of life in the prison shuffle? Have you asked Elohim for forgiveness, yet still walk in condemnation? Christ paid your debt, walk in victory.

He's the lifter of your head. Hold your head up!

He breaks every chain. Shake yourself loose!

Claim your conversion. Proclaim your pardon!

Be free indeed!

Have a Radiant Day!

Randi Meacham

About the Author

Randi is a Tennessee native with a passion for seeing women walking in freedom. Randi serves as a crisis advocate for women of sexual and domestic abuse and volunteers as a biblical life coach. The revelation of her true identity in the Most High has catapulted her from the comfort of complacency. Far too often, she has seen women delivered from shame and condemnation only to witness them fall back into the pit of brokenness.

Through the conviction of the Holy Spirit, she has accepted the call to proclaim the praises of Him who called her out of darkness into the marvelous light and to mentor women to do the same. Randi has been married to the love of her life for 30 years and is the mother of 3 sons and grandmother of 4 grandchildren.

Made in the USA
Middletown, DE
15 July 2021